Withinity

Withinity

John Patrick Whooley

Withinity Press

WITHINITY

KDP ISBN: 9798340844057

Why Withinity?

October 18th, 2024

Dear Reader,

All I know is what has worked for me.

Through an unwavering dedication to healing and after years of much suffering, I have found myself existing in a state of almost complete wellness, peace and fulfillment. There is no way to tell if this is to continue indefinitely, but the feeling in my heart says that it will. My desire is to share this place with you...

Intention and Invitation

My personal knowing is that we are and always have been complete, whole, and one with The Creator; and that every soul consciously and/or subconsciously desires to resolve what stands in the way of that truth being fully realized.

This perspective, combined with the Somatic Forgiveness process, has been a crucial part of my journey. Somatic Forgiveness uses uncomfortable feelings in the body to access the origin of limited beliefs, which then can be cleared through awareness, prayer, and surrendering to Source.

(for more on the process, please see the information at the end of the book or visit www.somaticforgiveness.com).

Therefore, Withinity is not just a book of spiritual thought. It is also intended as a container for community, and a process for healing.

I invite you to join me.

Sincerely,

John Patrick Whooley

P.S. Although I initially wrote this book for others, I now realize that it was also written as a reminder to myself.

Acknowledgements

I would like to thank the following people for their influence and/or assistance. If it were not for you, I would not be where I am today.

John Whooley Sr, Mary Aquinas Whooley, Aine McClafferty, Isadore Kelly, Mary Angela Whooey, Patricia Kulawiak, James Whooley, Monica Whooley, Gabriel Whooley, Moriah Melin, Patricia Clarke, Julietta St. John, Erin Hillary, Chiyan Wang, David Reynolds, John Newton, Bill Harris, Jacque Jefferies, Sue Mason, John Whoolilurie, Mary Whoolilurie, Adam Martone, Andrea Martone, Melissa Soltero, Chris Morgan, Pete Muller, Mark Fischer, Carrie Fisher, Christi Gubser, Tim Demme, Helen Highwater, Alicia Michelsen, Laura Haver, Dan Robbins, Gabriel Gage, Karen Jew, Tim Smolens, Jason Schimmel, Timb Harris, Dave Murray, Poco Marshall, Ramin Akbarnia, Max Katz, Mitra Tredway, Patrick Blue, Michael Holmes, George Smith, Bobby Weinstein, Vince Palmieri, Basil Webb, Robin Reynolds, Paul Contos, Will Hendren, and many others.

Thank you...

To Andrea

please read slowly

begin where you'd like

finish as you are

we have names

    yet how can we name the unnamable?

names point us in a direction

    that direction is within

all that is within

    and all that is without has the same origin

connection to source is

    and always has existed

        right before our eyes

close your eyes

    be still and see

without up there is no down

without dark there is no light

without in there is no out

for what is behind the two?

it is the One

let us remember

knowing a beginning will end

knowing day will become night

knowing everything in the material will go away

what remains?

Source

Love

Home

Forever

source is

  always has been

    always will be

disguised within everything and all

constantly giving

  loving

    perpetually receiving

      composting

        taking us home

without effort it nourishes and guides us

  while allowing for our own will and way

clear your burden so we all can see

does the collective agreement
   that influences the quantum field
     producing what we call reality
       nurture us in the deepest way?

do money, possessions, fame and entertainment
   provide any lasting joy
     or do they reinforce separation
       superiority and lack?

for when we lie on our deathbed, none of it will matter
   all that will remain is how we feel
     about ourselves and our relationships

how we loved
   how we forgave
     how we healed
       how we corrected our inner and outer worlds

that is the only judgment
   the judgment of ourselves

Source loves us infinitely

    patiently awaiting our return

        no matter how long it takes

resolve the judgments of your own heart

the Light of God is pouring through us all in equal measure

there is no difference between you and me
   us and them
      animal and human
         plant and creature
         rock and water

then why so much pain?

the Light interacts with unresolved burden
   creating the fire of suffering
      an alchemical process

eliminate karmic burden
   eliminate resistance
      eliminate suffering

Father/Mother Oneness

she gives
  allows
    and loves

because it is the One
  both sides of two belong to it
    and are accepted as family

the father loves the "bad" child equally to the "good" one
  the mother feeds the lost and the found
    knowing that return is inevitable for all

there is no way to fully understand

surrender and feel Her love

the stars rotate around the north star

   the spring wells up from under a rock

      the pinecone has its center

         the wheel moves due to the space at its core

         all revolves around the center point

let us stay there

we can call it Mother

  loving

    caring

      providing

        allowing

          birthing

we can call it Father

  focused

    impregnating

      pumping

        giving

          taking action

gender isn't accurate here

  for unity has no gender

we can call it Home

are you homesick

longing to return?

we use senses to glimpse and feel that place for a moment

but it won't last

by clearing burden

and preparing the field for the seeds of truth to grow

we move towards liberation

awareness allows us to be at home

while away

on this adventure called human life

how do I want to be?

    I want to be like God

effortless

    at peace

        forgiving

            allowing

                detached

                    available

                        complete

                        giving

                            receiving

                        perpetually loving

imitation is the highest form of flattery

Masters such as Jesus, Buddha, Krishna, Lao-tzu, and others

    became this

the essence

    the example

        the ideal

            not the idol

positive thinking
  intention
    and emotionally resonating with our desired future
      it is so necessary and valuable

however
  without preparing the field
    how can our garden properly produce and grow?

clear the burden
  resolve the past
    forgive yourself
      forgive all

then the field will be ready for the seeds of healthy creation

the outside is the inside

what we see and experience in the world
   is a reflection of ourselves

     the world is a mirror
       our inner sight is a mirror

anything that makes us uncomfortable
   that creates opposition
     that can be seen as conflict
       is illusion

let it be resolved

before we breathe air
  we breathe water

the void is like an endless sea
  perfectly still
    until the most subtle of influence creates a current
      which then builds upon itself

let us be like water

receptive
  patient
    cleansing
      clear
        adaptive
          responsive

for we are water
  we are nature

    let us emulate that in our lives
      existing in the original state of being

why rush ahead?

   the turtle wins the race

allow for the current of God

all will be cared for

the power and magnificence of the Consciousness

   that guides billions of people

      to receive exactly what they need

        at the perfect time

           as all lives interweave seamlessly

            is beyond comprehension

I praise the Gentle Magnificence

   and Power of the Creator

effortlessly

   peacefully

      and perfectly

        caring for all

can we learn when to stop
   can we step back at the perfect moment?
     for if we push
       might we eventually lose our balance and fall?

when is enough?

we will know
   if our sight is clear

in stillness the debris of the mind will settle

then we can see
   hear
     and feel Her message

knowing we are truly that

the in-between

access the in-between
music, laughter, togetherness, love
concerts, celebrations, shows, movies
or alcohol, drugs, food, screens and more

access the in-between
slip into that place of connection
with ourselves
with others
with God

let us see all activities as divine
though some with a cost

till the garden
so we can perpetually reside
in the in-between

we exist in the mind of God

the consciousness looking out of your eyes
   is the same consciousness looking out of mine

if there is only one
   then we are all a part
     and have equal claim to God Consciousness

make thine eye single
  and look past thought
    without division or separation

I am thought and now I rest
  effortlessly
    patiently
      perfectly

be in and of that place

it may appear difficult
  but approach with ease

like a deer resting in the meadow

bring effortlessness to our lives
  our minds
    our bodies
      our relationships

see the outside as a reflection of the inside

peace and perfection

    not opposition and challenge

        restore what has always existed within

          and the outer world will resolve itself

the mind churns out thoughts
  some positive
    some neutral
      some negative

to achieve stillness
  allow thoughts to pass
    like people walking by in a crowded place

look beyond distraction
  concentrate until what was hidden becomes all there is

this is our true nature

when emptied

   space is created to receive

     to hold

       provide the container

        nothingness is our greatest treasure

         our truest nature

          a whisp of smoke penetrates the heavens

           with our prayers of surrender

let us rest there

then we can see

   feel and hear

     that we are that

are you restless

   do you crave entertainment?

what occurs if you sit without distraction

   what does your mind say

      how does your body feel?

deal with that reflection and find peace

correct mental errors

   to discover a deeper truth

      prepare to let go of that deeper truth

         if and when the next level of understanding emerges

let go to what is

   resolve discomfort as it comes

freedom

Jesus, Buddha, Lao-tzu
    Mary, Guanyin, Sophia
        Krishna, Yogananda, Hafiz

do you think yourself any less
    any different?

All is One

many of us believe it
    but do we feel it
        and know it
            with every cell of our body?

for once we do
    some may call that liberation

there is only One

if there is only One
  then you
     I
       everyone
         and everything
          is of that One

like flowers on the tree of God
  we blossom and bear fruit
    all in perfect time

if we are of the One Tree
  then we can see the world as ourselves

by finding peace within
  we make peace with the world
    for there is no separation

when we operate from a place of unity

    our lives become fulfilled

        complete

           peaceful

                and nourishing

true abundance is ours forever

I want peace for myself
  and for all

   by finding peace within
    I find it without

let us exist in the current of Peace

dis-eased thinking and action may be close
  but they pass on by
   for no resistance is offered
    I see it as an unresolved part of myself

correct observation keeps me safe

look forward to a future of effortlessly nourishing thoughts

it is our birthright

oh silly evil

   you sad little child

      you think you can win

         but you can't

you are losing control

   actually, you never had control

      is that why you are trying everything possible

         to divide and destroy?

         a narcissist thinks it can usurp the will of God

            that it is God

how gravely mistaken you are, my dear

just know you are forgiven

   as soon as you can forgive yourself

God unconditionally loves all of Her children

come home sweetie

is it an orb
  a ball
    a point
      a block
        the quantum field?

colorful but drab
  moving yet stationary
    all pervading but substance-less
      full but empty

paradoxically it is all these things
  and none of them

    without any possible opposite
      we can call it Home

what peace!

what subtleness and purpose
what a sense of being loved

for without you I am nothing
without you there is nothing

join me in drinking from the Divine

effortlessly
endlessly
for all is in the hands of the Creator

have the courage to cleanse illusion and resistance
so simple!

and although there was much suffering along the way
looking back now
it all seems so easy

an idol distracts from the ideal that exists within us all

seeing the anointed one we call Christ as an idol
    dilutes the power of the message

        hearing the name we call Buddha as separate from ourselves
            is illusion

            if they existed at all
                for how can we truly know?

if they did or did not exist
    they were open
        receptive
            forgiving
                loving
                    clear
                        shapeable
                            kind
                                and generous

they didn't expect or seek
    they knew they were found

let us be still

    let us settle

        for peace is achieved within

give God a clear vessel to speak through

the love of God is always present

it has
  is
    and always will be

how hilarious it was right in front of my eyes this whole time!

I've had many glimpses
  but again it would become hidden

    don't look for it in flash or sensation
      though those can be used to point the way

no one is any more or less worthy
  no one is any more or less special
    eventually all will return

so much peace in that

can you feel it
  know it
    and live from it fearlessly without weight?

cleanse and resolve what lies between us and Source

put others above and we place ourselves below

to become like them we must win
   which means others will lose

the advanced soul sees herself in all
   she doesn't give her gifts to some and not to others
     for there are no others

there is only God

we think we're so smart and we are!

the mind is great at a certain thing
   a thing called duality

therefore, we see danger instead of ourselves
   others instead of a mirror
     lack instead of wholeness
      and evil instead of our own shadow

let the heart lead

the law is written in our hearts

everyone knows what is correct action
the proper way to treat others
the proper way to treat ourselves

we will all be shown the error of our ways

let us emulate God

how can we?

let us imitate Her openness
　receptivity
　　and forgiveness

seeing all as part of ourselves

let us be infinite
　for we are

　　let us see no separation
　　　for there is none

　　　let us love the least
　　　　for we are them

　　　　let us not compete
　　　　　for competition with ourselves is an impossibility

I am thought
　you are thought
　　there is only thought

what happens when thought rests?

we return to our original state
　before the thought of creation

we may identify with thought
　however, when thought rests
　　we enter the collective mind of God
　　　of the All
　　　　of the One

then we are home
　though we never left

enjoy worldly things

  food

    music

      sense

        nature

          connection

          and family

see them for what they are

  manifestations of the One

enjoy in proper order

do you want it all?

  you already are it All

    what is it we resist

      that keeps us from embracing that completely?

let us give ourselves to our deficiencies

  let us clean the dust from our closets

    let us prepare the garden

positive thinking and intention is lost

  if the field of past karma is not weeded

prepare to receive the Word

are we holding on to possessions

  money

    status

      reputation?

for relying on the world

  a transitory experience

    is holding on to illusion and provides no real security

hold on to the unchangeable love-mirror
    you see when you close your eyes
        for when we care only for the Tao
            all within and all without is cared for

how can we trust this?
    by unlearning
        by surrendering
            by following
                by resting

we are nature

when the storm comes
  don't resist

emotion is healthy
  anger is healthy
    storms are healthy

they cleanse, reset, express and allow

we get into trouble when we don't allow them to pass
  when we hold on

let us make ourselves one with nature

can fire mean purification rather than destruction
  can melting ice mean a revealing rather than doom
    can we merge with the wisdom of nature?

for nature knows without comprehending
  expresses without thought

be whole

    there is nothing else

resolve anything standing in the way of truth

the standard agreement in our current time
  of how to operate in life
    to succeed and stay safe
      is to push ahead
        and work harder than the other
          to dominate

this approach leaves others behind

if others are us
  then we limit ourselves
    while reinforcing separation and duality

temporary wins and victories are based in delusion
  they leave us wanting more
    feeling lack
      desperation
        and fear
          for it all will go away

let us drop into the current of the Lord
  the speed of the Divine

personal yet impersonal
   unchanging yet fluid
      solitary yet receptive

it knows all because it is All

we give it a name but it is beyond name
   we give it a shape but it is beyond shape
      it is our Mother but that doesn't describe it
         it is our Father but that doesn't fully express

its power is beyond comprehension
   it loves and allows us
      we are its most revered children

which of our insights are filtered

    through the lens of untrue history?

        how can we know in actuality how we came to be?

investigate

    while accepting the possibility of never truly knowing

        and that what we have been taught could be false

masters I adore and respect

    transmit information that to me seems partially incorrect

can different interpretations of particular concepts be resolved

    can insights, which have fundamental truths imbedded

        be skewed or misinterpreted?

and then

    what is it that I am missing, seeing or interpreting incorrectly

        how are my understandings filtered through conditioning?

I vow to release any beliefs that are proven to be false

    no matter how truthful and integrated they seemed before

then I stay like a little child

immersed in the wonder

the unfathomable power

peace and magnificence

of the Tao

could it be

that humans are the only beings that can reflect
    that we are it
        of it
            and that there is nothing else?

we are flowers on its tree
    waves on its ocean
        grapes on its vine

what an honor to know that what I see
    both within and without
        I Am

cleanse the mirror that you are

let us imitate God

   let us be all potential

      why choose who we are?

         leave that up to the Master

I allow myself to be formed from the block

the sun shines in the sky
  giving to all
    creating all
      feeding all
        nourishing all

but behind it is darkness
  the stationary and unmoving nothingness
    that is home to the light

therefore

let us feel the sun
  embrace human existence
    be present with family
      honor the children
        watch them play

enjoy this life
  but remember the darkness...
    the constant and complete connection
      to the stationary and unchanging unity
        which supports and maintains all

upon his deathbed a friend proclaimed
   "it's so obvious!"

The Great Mother
   The Kingdom

connection to home is completely available and always present
   it has never been apart from you
      disguised in plain sight
         and pointed to through feeling

the perfect Light of God is skewed
   through the unclean lens of karma and burden

resolve and restore
   so we may clearly see
      what is
         and what has always been

why wait until our dying breath?
   do it now

let us emulate God

loving
  receptive
    allowing
      forgiving
        peaceful

let us see everyone and everything
  as a reflection of ourselves

is it possible...
  that when we become completely healed
    the outside world will become so as well?

can we move forward without attachment
  can we change course
    when life shows us a new correct action
    can we let go of beliefs
      if they are shown to be conceived in error?

can we settle into the ever-available current of the Lord

    can we completely dedicate ourselves to truth

      to what is

        to the mysteries of the Master?

can we choose a meaning that verifies all?

yes we can

after one comes two

expression of the two is a dance pointing to the one

the block
   the field
      all possibility
         is the female

the point
   the sun
      the edge
         is the male

the male demonstrates as the action needed for creation

but when we choose a particularity
   we exclude all other possibilities

let us stick to the block

    while knowing how to act

        or better yet

            allow our actions to be chosen by the Lord

                let our free will be His

true freedom

then we remain in the realm of potential

    allowing ourselves to adapt and react to every situation

        accepting the world as it is

            responding perfectly and as needed

                always and forever

could it be that the world is perfect

could any sense of wrongness

be seen only through our own lens?

could all the trials of life

be a necessary and natural part of this human experience?

danger/safety

exhaustion/vigor

conflict/peace

failure/success

behind/ahead

let us see every moment as part of the whole

of the journey

there are storms

hills

difficulty

ease

relief

and arrival

all necessary parts of a good journey

    of a good story

        of a good song

do not allow ease or difficulty

    to define or add meaning to who and what you are

who are you

what are you?

as we surrender to the will of God

and eliminate any distortion of that message

a moment arrives where there is no more need to push

control

resist

or fight

for any aggressive or controlling action

will only rebound upon itself

causing suffering

the greatest evil is defeated through surrender

for evil exists as an opposition

if it has no opposition

it has no power

of course, a reaction in the moment may be necessary

but let us eliminate any frequency or belief

that would attract it into our lives

all rivers lead to the sea

its power is in its acceptance of what is
  its ability to absorb
    hold
      contain
        and allow for any condition

it has infinite capacity to cleanse and renew
  create and cradle

such peaceful power

we are all heading in that direction
  homecoming is inevitable

to engage in violence

what a tragedy

for it is ourselves we are in battle with

an external version of the war within

let us conquer the within

the hardest battle

for once it is won

where all aspects emerge victorious

and there is no loser

it all will have seemed so effortless and perfect

let us realize there does exist an agenda

from within and without

that drives us towards separation

let us love it as the prodigal son

can we forgive the most evil of hearts?

for those souls need it the most

underneath all of that darkness

   is the heart of a little child that needs love

can we feel at home
   while away on this human experience?

home is perfect
   stationary
      endlessly renewing
         perpetually giving

it is Heaven
   haven
      safety

see inner and outer vision as ourselves
   the entire ocean exists within the single drop
      a drop of peace
         of stillness
            of love

created in its image are we
   created in its ideal is the earth

say it

I Am One with the All

all answers are found within

    all wisdom is available

when direct knowledge resonates

    with what we encounter without

        we have a confirmation

however, let us not cling

    for one concept that now seems true

        may fade away with the integration of new information

it was a necessary step

    on the path of internal and external investigation

stay with source

    observe

        follow the manifestations

            but hold to the wellspring

the smallest bit of poisoning at the fountainhead

    pollutes the demonstration

clean

   allow

      look within

see without as within

   stay with Source

      all will resolve

Dear God,

I am so amazed by your love
   your power and humility
      your acceptance and gentleness
         your loving awareness

every step of my life has been guided
   seamlessly integrated with my free will

and in every step
   I received exactly what I needed
      for healing
         growth
            and evolution

this is occurring for every human
   animal
      creature
         and thing

in a web of allowing that weaves all lives together perfectly so vast

   and unimaginable

     so complete

       beautiful

        and perfect

thank you...

hidden
  silent
    still

mundane
  dull
    perfect

soft
  slow
    complete

peaceful
  stationary
    loving

always giving
  giving always
    in all ways

notice...

be like this

    for it is what you are

be yourself

water dissolves the stone
  essence penetrates the rigid

   softness always wins
    for it is in no rush

let us illuminate what we wish to resolve
  let us allow what doesn't serve us to be seen and honored

there was a time when those beliefs and actions
  were appropriate and wise
   but no longer

can we see a negative thought, action or habit
  as a perfect expression of the Divine?
   for it is

once it has been seen
  heard
   validated
    and loved
     it can rest
      knowing its job is done

it's Yin Yang Day!

let us give what we have received
    so others may benefit from what has been bestowed upon us

as we allow for this outward flow of grace
    we make room for more within ourselves
        what we then receive will only complement and compound
            upon what we have already been given

the cycle continues

in one way it builds
    in another way it clears and empties
        both at the same time

flow
    breath
        heartbeat

and behind it is the One

where is heaven?

  this is Heaven

for when we emulate the Tao

  we become peaceful

    tolerant

     dignified

     patient

      understanding

      and radiant

so too will our earth

  when allowed to return to its natural state

   become full

    abundant

     giving

      nourishing

       supportive

       balanced

       and endlessly renewed

for it already is

a haven

    Heaven

It begins within

    and manifests without

desire only the will of God and you will find peace

Oh Master
   Lord
      Mother
         Father,

I love you

I feel you loving me always and completely

what a joy
   what an honor!

I allow you to guide my every step

thank you...

all I want is to help
   all I want is to give
      for in giving I receive

shape me
   use me
      let me be like You

quiet yet always available
   beautiful without attempt or effort
      receptive to all in need
         giving without expectation
            willing to correct all mistakes and misconceptions
               tolerant and loving to all
                  a pure and complete channel of peace

realize you are all
    and you will always have enough

        reach for more and lose
            never to be satisfied

            the current of love exists and leads
                gently and perfectly

                if we swim against it
                    we won't arrive at the perfect time!

to enter the current
    surrender

surrender your body
    mind
        spirit
            expectations
                presuppositions
                and desires

become the desire behind all desire

   our deepest need

      our deepest calling

to go Home

She says

"Come home to me
   I can wait forever

      you are always welcome
         you have always been loved

however you want to approach
   whether straightforward or crooked
      long or short
         I am here loving you
            guiding you gently with allowance
               your only need is to forgive yourself

I have never held anything against you
   how can I hold anything against myself?

for you are of me and there is nothing else, my child"

we experience opposites

they may seem extreme
   though two sides of the same coin

simplicity is the undercurrent
  peace is the virtue
    the simplest explanation is most often correct

we search for answers
  giving away our power to experts
    forgoing our own intelligence
      so we can be told what to think
        feel
          and do

there is but one expert
  you and I are extensions of that expert

remember your proper place

do not believe anything learned from teachers

  books

    history

      the news

        or religion

          unless that information resonates

          with our own interpretation

          and integration of the data

if the information from within

  resonates with what we encounter without

    and we have done our best

      to clear our inner sight of illusion

        then we can make a decision of what is

even then, hold the possibility of changing our minds

  if or when convincing and proper evidence presents itself

be like water

  the water in which you came

could it be

   that God

      in its formless state

         thought itself into created form

            in its own image

               complete and whole

                  perpetually existing?

completion was then split

Yin and Yang

   male and female

      light and dark

         was born

the wheel began to spin

   from two a third was born

      from there all creation ensued

imagine your body

a vessel

  a cup

    a container

however, what you really are

  is the space the container holds

is your water clear

  are there any dyes

    is there any pollution

      illusion

        or resistance?

for if there is

  as the Light of God shines through

    it will hit that pollution

skewing

  refracting

    and darkening the light we emit

when we clean the vessel

   and purify our water

      the light shines through

         as intended

pure

   clear

      and perfect

this is our true nature

through stillness

   surrender

      acceptance

         and softness

            all is accomplished

            all is reconciled

let us relax

   into complete and total union with the Creator

      there is nothing to be done

         for it is already done

all glory to the Master

why do we want to be seen

   why do we want recognition

      does it come from a place of lack

         are we indirectly grasping for our parent's attention

            for God's attention

               for love?

are we acting from a place of believing love is conditional?

we choose these experiences

   God chooses these experiences through us

just so we can remember

   that we are

      completely

         and unconditionally

            loved

can you trust the world

  are you safe?

    if the answer is no

      then is it possible you don't trust yourself?

       there is only one path

        though many detours

        it is called return

we can witness our own

  but can we see theirs?

stop

  be still

    see the inevitability

help those who ask

  have compassion for those who don't

    let them react to you

      while finding amusement at their confusion

for your light is seen through a cloudy lens

they won't understand

let them judge

Dear God,

my only desire is to be with You

let me purify myself to where there can be no more doubt
    fear
       or resistance

let me see everything and everyone
    as a representation of You and I
       of the All

I give it all to you

do you have an enemy?

I am sorry if you do

for the enemy is yourself projected into the outside world
    all we encounter are versions of ourselves

can we love them
    forgive them
        and help them
            without self-sacrifice?

can we love ourselves
    forgive ourselves
        help ourselves?

the master's baseline is peace
    any seeming opposition is only shadow

return to truth

I love you

sit still

  close your eyes

    hear your thoughts

can you see them as well?

how was creation created before the Word?

  it was Thought

ask "as thought, can I rest?"

our thoughts are not to battle

  to be in conflict with

let us merge and realize

  that thought is all there is

    the source of creation

surrender to the will of God

  surrender to yourself

    surrender to the Father

    surrender to Hymn

there is nothing to say

silence is the deepest connection
   thoughtlessness is union
      I want to rest there

yet there is a job to be done
   and in that job words are needed

I purify my vessel so there can be no chance of distortion

we often say "everything happens for a reason"

    or "wow, what a coincidence!"

        or "I was thinking of you when you called"

           or "what did that dream mean?"

none of this comes as a surprise

    for it is all God

the more we see

    trust

        and feel this,

           the more we can accept

               and cannot deny

until finally we arrive at full integration

    the beginning and the ending

let every man honor the feminine

for without her
    nothing is possible

every woman is the Divine Mother
    every man is the Divine Father
        Yin and Yang wants to unite

do not confuse this desire with sex
    though in ways it is one and the same

the masculine leads
    but only with the permission of
        and in surrender to
            the feminine

Dear God,

with the deepest humility and intention
   I lay my every step
      thought
         action
            and breath
               in your hands

thank you...

God has His way

evil

   which some call the narcissist mind

      is completely blind to the fact that it works for Love

its desperation is an indication

   of its inevitable loss of power and control

      the narcissist hates that

try as it may to stop it

   the water will eventually find its way to the ocean

are you afraid to die

  do you lament aging

    do you feel dis-ease existing in the manifest world?

let us clean our vessel

  purify our mind

so information

  insight

    and the light of God can come through unaltered

let the light burn away all resistance

  delusion

    burden

      illusion

        and distortion

until all that is left

  is a perfect

    clean

      pure

        and receptive vessel

let us be born again

then we will know and feel

   without doubt

      without a shadow of a doubt

      that we will live forever

we are all celebrating God
   whether we know it or not

every bird that sings
   every deer that leaps
      every moment of eye contact
         or laughter at the bar

all connection and expression is a celebration of the Lord
   a celebration of the ever loving and ever giving joy
      that perpetually exists

we think it's the food or drink
   music or show
      yoga or joke

however
   those only allow access to what is already there
      a love waiting to be embraced
         experienced and felt

our Great Mother is caring for us

    guiding us

        protecting us

            and allowing us to learn our own lessons

expectantly

    yet patiently awaiting our return

come home my love

    come home

perceived was an epic battle between good and evil

it was waged in the place of the in-between
one turn of the wheel was 24,000 years

I do not know this for a fact

I sided with good
preparing to defend myself and those that I love
ready to fight to the death
ritualistically and with honor

I then realized that victory would come only through surrender
nonviolence
forgiveness
allowing
and having compassion for the narcissist mind

the wheel stopped
all found peace

will the cycle start again?
I do believe so

however and once again

   the victory

      where all win and are cared for

         is inevitable

shhhhhhhh...

in the darkness there is light

    a light that mirrors the Creator as well as ourselves

through the narrow gate we see beyond the light

    into the stillness behind the action

        the darkness behind the flame

stationary

    unified

        indivisible oneness

            peace

              home

                love

God

    Father

        Mother

            Creator

let us clear our vessel

   so our desires are in line with those of the Master

    so our free will becomes the will of God

paradoxically we become the creator of our own lives

   while always maintaining proper relationship to the Boss

allow things to take care of themselves

    shape the current by not interfering

surrender to the Great Will

    Plan

       and Way

why resist?

    it only causes suffering

      face discomfort and pain to transcend limitation

        for it is only a feeling in the body

the pain of finding the courage to forgive ourselves is short lived

    compared to a loop of lifetimes rehashing the same story

there is a natural way

a current
  a flow
    a great river

a river that runs deep and wide and true
  emptying into the sea

yet curiosity and ego invite us to take the side streams

in those branches
  we accumulate mud
    get stuck
      and extend the journey

we are slowed down
  become homes for creatures
    ideas
      concepts
        and limitations

stay in the current or choose the side streams

which path do you choose?

reality is sustained by vibration

sound
  music
    the Word
      Om
        Aum
         Hymn

we are emitting a frequency
  based on our past burden and experience

that frequency resonates with the outside world
  attracting the same level of relationship
    money
      connection to God
        connection to ourselves

until we clean our garden
  house
    closet
      and field
        we will subconsciously attract limited levels

resolve your burden

    while embracing that all experience

        has been chosen and self-created

freedom awaits

The Church of Iesa

  The Dead Sea Scrolls

    Astrotheology

      the Essenes

        the many times the story has appeared before

it is logically quite possible that Jesus never historically existed

  and quite possible that he did

    who knows?

      how liberating!

complete and direct connection to God

  then becomes available to us all

we are all the Iesa Crios

did I spell that right?

if we accept every situation

how can we suffer?

if we are unoffendable

how can we be hurt

if we see all as ourselves

why would we need to shine?

if we emulate water

we can conform to any container

and adapt to every situation

if our only desire is to be like the Tao

we then become eternal

for it is what we have always been

if we have nothing to prove

we can stay quiet

if we are available

then all can receive our support

the law is written in our hearts
  the way appears by itself
    the first step reveals the pathway home

when we tell people what to do
  how to be
    or which path to take
      they resist

for everyone needs to discover it for themselves

correct action is written in our hearts
  just observe a small child and a puppy
    playing in the grass

as above so below

as within so without

the turning of the stars is a clock

what we see and encounter in the world is a mirror

the meaning we apply to the manifest

is insight to how we perceive ourselves

do you see danger or harmony

do you see opposition or yourself

do you trust and love the least

or do you judge them and feel aversion?

cleanse yourself

prepare your vessel to receive the Lord

don't try to be beautiful

  you are beautiful

    just allow it to express

      perfectly imperfect as you are

        as all begins with thought

          so does your beauty and radiance

cleanse your inner world

  weed your garden

    compassionately confront ideas and perceptions

      make sure they are true

        accept what is

          no matter how it differs from what others may think

allow truth to emerge from the wellspring of your being

your most beautiful version will demonstrate

  in your physical relationships and manifestations

    and in relationship to yourself

don't forget

you were made in the image of the Creator

express

  then release

    respond

      then be quiet

        allow the current to guide your every step

be what you are

  nature

storms come and go

  rain pours then stops

    clouds form then pass

the sun's intensity varies throughout the day

  throughout the seasons

    water takes the path of least resistance

      and accepts all circumstance

      how patient can you be

        how faithful?

let us consider the mystery of the feminine

   as Holy Mary Mother of God

the sun is our life-giving energy

   but the infinite feminine field of possibility

     supports and nourishes all

       including the son

Father Seed and Mother Field

but behind it all

Oneness

  Nothingness

   All-ness

     (   )

       enter unknowable name above

everything that has ever happened

   has been perfectly guided and allowed

     by the effortless plan of the Creator

every encounter

   conversation

     bird

       cat

         and child

every disruption

   illness

     conflict

       and success

         is a message and reflection from the Divine

have seemingly negative occurrences

   turned out to be exactly what was needed

     leading us to our current path?

the more we shed resistance to what is

    the more accepting and receptive we become

        the more we can yield and surrender

            the more we see the perfection that has always been

I bow with awe

    to the consciousness that guides and accomplishes all

        all without a plan

every hair on your head is numbered

I do not deny the existence of evil
however, I like to call it by a different name
the narcissist mind

one that believes itself superior to
and more important than all else
including God

is it possible that the language of spells
has been used to program the collective consciousness
that all is the woman's fault?
evil
Eve is ill

coincidence?
is there even such a thing?

for such a tragedy manifests
as the programming that the feminine
is responsible for the fall of man

let us see the narcissist mind for what it is
a sad child who needs compassion, love and attention

step out of it's way

    love it as it passes by

        see it as a potentially unresolved place in yourself

recognize the power of nonviolence

surrender is power
  humility is leadership
    patience is supreme

let us not cling to any idea
  but be open to all correction
    let us consider another as ourselves
      so we can learn from every situation

let us see the enemy as our greatest teacher
  for it is our own shadow

see how much you've learned and grown?

every thought

  word

    deed

      and action

        is of the Tao

incorrect action is necessary

  for it guides us to the path of return

resolve any idea or feeling that God is judging you

  that there is anything anyone needs to do

    to be received in the Father's house

forgive yourself

  correct your thoughts

    words

      and actions

be one with Home

when something arises is there resistance or acceptance?
life presents what needs to be addressed

bring awareness to this constantly giving well
within and without

be available to the moment's necessity
to circumstances
people
and nature

for when we avoid
conflict is created
throwing off the balance

if we correct ourselves in the moment
there is little difficulty
if we let avoidance grow
resolving becomes a larger effort

tend to your garden when the weeds first appear
more effort is required once roots have grown

and while present with every action

   keep your mind with Hymn

      it will give you peace

         purpose and pause

this is my own advice to myself

when we as thought rest

    we return to our primordial identity

like a baby in the womb

before any hints of language take form

    in the place of unity with the Mother

        both in the physical and in the Divine

the simplicity of form

it springs from the center point

we see it manifested in nature
   machine
    people
     the eye
      all of creation

let us direct desire towards becoming that form
   for we already are

by correcting
   forgiving
    and resolving everything up until that point

we cannot attain Centerpointe
   but we can join Hymn
    at the right hand of the Father
     at the left hand of the Mother

knowledge or wisdom?

knowledge can be seen as understanding the ways of the world

   knowledge of facts and figures

     places and stories

       information about things that will all change or go away

wisdom is cultivated over lifetimes

   in resonance with

     the unchangeable and omnipresent Oneness

knowledge needs to be relearned or reminded of

   wisdom evolves and compounds forever

seek wisdom

there is a grand plan

settle into the current
   resolve any frequency of doubt
      embrace patience

the wheel of time
   the map of the stars
      the clock of God
         is in perpetual motion
            allowed by stillness

to make life's timing about us is a disconnect from proper order

surrender to the Master

I humble myself to God

I humble myself to you

there is an infinite amount to learn from you
   for you are the same divine expression as am I

if our paths are destined to cross
   there must be a reason
      lesson
        benefit
          and purpose

there is but one path
   the path of return

      returning to what is
         what has always been

            that we never left home
               we just couldn't feel it

I make way for you

    please pass in peace

        I surrender

the countless trinities

the archetype of the pyramid
    holding so much meaning and significance

stability
    strength
        and support

and its foundational relationship to the capstone

let us be simple
    efficient
        reserved
            accepting
                and allowing

let us be compassionate
    though without empathy
        holding space and wishing resolution for all
            while taking on no weight
                or burden

all is in God's hands

do we operate from a place of what is best for all

    or do we put ourselves above the others we interact with?

for others are us and we are them

the enemy is our own shadow

    the opponent is our reflection

let us play to win

    but accept loss graciously

        realizing we are all on the same team

we will never comprehend
  the magnificence and power of the Tao

it perfectly guides without interfering
  allowing us to find our own way home
    it trusts in our nature
      for we are of and completely that

        and though we will never truly understand
          we can eliminate all that stands in the way
            of becoming it completely
              for we already are it completely

let us peacefully and perfectly live the simple and practical life
  becoming who we are meant to be
    a servant of the Master and Her plan

look inside your heart
  be patient and wait
    all will be revealed

I see the great wheel of time turning
   Unity stepped down from its original state of perfection

    duality was born
     allowed by the Creator

the battle of good and evil
   the dance of light and dark
    the wheel of Yin and Yang

    darkness is not inherently evil
     light is not inherently good

in perceiving the inevitable attack of evil
   we prepare to defend ourselves

we see the opponent as another
   but the enemy is ourselves
    unresolved burden reflects this

when good surrenders to evil and turns the other cheek
   the battle ceases to exist

surrender is the most powerful action

or may we say, non-action?

yielding is the most sacred virtue

or may we say, non-virtue?

nothing to say

  nothing to do

    nothing to teach

      nothing to share

let us arrive at non-action

watch in wonder as God takes care and accomplishes all

  without effort

    in complete peace

      and in perfect timing

all is reconciled

hidden

  but omnipresent

    silent

      but emanating the Word that sustains all realities

always giving

  always loving

    always joyful

      always receiving

        through thoughtless awareness

          all is accomplished

            guided

            and completed

it gently contains all

  stretching and contracting so perfectly

    that most don't even notice

let us rest in the mystery

we cannot know the magnificence
  the power
    the plan

we may have ideas
  or a direction
    signs
      and a calling

but if things don't turn out as we expect
  can that be accepted completely
    knowing all is cared for?

all is well
  all is a well
    all is good
      all is God

can we see perfection
  in the manifestations we normally call bad or wrong?

may anything standing in the way of complete realization

be resolved and reconciled

as we look into the mirror we call the "real world"
  we see things that can be interpreted as bad or wrong

there is a force that exists
  the narcissist mind
    more commonly known as evil

although it is allowed by God
  and works for God
    it doesn't see it
      because it is ill

this dis-ease is called grandiosity

as we see it demonstrating
  in more and more blatant ways
    please don't fear for your safety
      rather, see it as a sign
        that the narcissist mind is losing control

in the infinite darkness
  the light will always prevail
    for its foundation is rooted in darkness

all things change
   all things go away
     all life dies

you will die
   I will die

live from this place and be free

eliminate anything that presents this as burden
   rather than liberation

although I feel at peace in human form
   I do look forward to returning to Forever
     when my work is done

the greatest of teachers realize there is nothing to teach
   they know that subtracting is far more valuable than adding

      but no teaching helps us unlearn
         we must embark upon that journey for ourselves

any and all intermediaries
   religion, authority or government
      institutions, history and programming
         need to be seen for what they truly are

arrows that point back to ourselves
   as the authority of wisdom and understanding

for the answers are within
   that there is only God
      love
         truth
            and peace

a holy love

   a holy truth

      a holy peace

The Holy Trinity

look within

   see for yourself

Dear Infinite Creator,

guide my every step

I am everything
   but nothing without you

thank you...

be like God

    take care of yourself

be like the Tao

    expect nothing of others

be like the Great Mother

    love and allow all

be like our Father in Heaven

    awaiting the prodigal son's return

be like the Infinite Creator

    rest in your perfection

be like Love

    leave people alone

let us be flexible

   so when life brings its storms

      we bend like a willow in the wind

let us be youthful in spirit

   so no preconceived notion

      can restrict us from embracing what is

live forever

I see you rushing about
    but are you getting ahead
        leaving others behind?

don't define, release
    don't try, be
        don't attach, accept
            don't push, relax
                don't avoid, resolve

step off the edge and surrender to the current
    the current moment

it is
    has
        and always will be available

hear it
    see it
        feel it
            be it

there is no one better than anyone else

no one more

no one less

there is only one path

the path of return

a path that leads towards God-Realization

and although no one is better

and no one is worse

there are those who are farther along

see the least as the most

for there is no difference

receive as much as you give

be loved as much as you love

allow balance to exist in all aspects of your life

internally

externally

as a leader

and as a follower

Oneness gives birth to Yin and Yang

may your expression of Yin Yang honor and express
the Unity that you truly are

flexible
    receptive
        yielding
            allowing
                cleansing

water

it dissolves
    shapes
        carves
            and creates

as above so below

we were created in water and of water
    we return to the water of the waters

        slow and soft
            is more effective than fast and hard

all is achieved through patience

be like water

be yourself

settle into the container provided by God

do what is asked

dissolve the inflexible

be one with the Creator

for you already are

sacred, scared
　divine, devil
　　bless, be less
　　　pray, prey
　　　　hello, hell
　　　　　who put the fun in funeral?!

what exists behind these extremes?

for if we lean into one, the other is created

nothing is any more of less sacred
　all is equally special and completely of God

although there is no superiority

    there is advanced and less advanced

        more or less evolved

the advanced soul realizes

    that she has invited every experience into her life

        that mistakes are lessons

            and that sins (missing the mark)

                are opportunities to correct behavior

                not vehicles for shame and guilt

free from weight

    karma

        and burden

            the advanced know they are not perfect

            though they strive to be

if you see a reason

    please correct me

        I invite all accurate reflection

the joy of feeling at home while in human form
   wants to be shouted from the rooftops
      for it is everyone's birthright and eventuality

others in peril are only earlier versions of ourselves

it is our job to help
   to share
      to unite

I want nothing else

is there anything more beautiful than the simple life?

family
  friends
    work
      play
        children
          nature
            connection
          and joy?

we so often embark on the journey of discovery
  longing
    desire
      and ego

only to realize
  that home is where we are most at peace

    align yourselves with the Tao
      stay home

all glory to Hymn
   there is only Hymn
      I am completely of Hymn
         as are you

can you feel it
   know it
      and be it?

so easy
   so simple

feel the mystery of the feminine nourishing and protecting us

She's got our back
    while the focused male energy of action is directed forward

in that intersection of male and female
    in that transitionary place
        Unity occurs

there we are complete
    perfect
        unified
            and One

what a beautiful place to reside
    let us stay there

simple
  truthful
    patient
      loving
        giving
          surrendering all

adapting
  bending
    accepting
      surrounding
        cleansing
          and slowing

I allow myself to be taken by the current

serving
  trusting
    seeing myself in all
      knowing without understanding

this is my only desire

it has been suggested

   that God created in order experience duality

     which is ultimately itself

are we the only beings

   that are aware of existence

     and can state

       I AM?

our consciousness is the consciousness of the Creator

   individuated into our seemingly separate forms

we are existing in

   of

     and as the mind of God

anything that leads us to believe otherwise is delusion

   and is based on unresolved karma and burden

therefore

    incarnations are the path to eventual return

       to the truth that there is only One

          and that we are all completely of that One

            and there is nothing else...

Rejoice!

be what you are in essence

perfect
  whole
    complete
      loving
        One with All

apply this insight to all you encounter
  let yourself be an example
    by not doing a thing

allow things to take care of themselves

to feel you so deeply is such an honor

I accept any and all accurate correction
   I know my place and take no credit
      I am your humble servant

use me
   guide me
      embody me

I feel your love
   personal yet indifferent

I am a tiny point of your expression
   yet I feel your constant presence and attention
      flowing in and out of me like a perpetually producing well

I give the same back to you
   for my ultimate desire is to be like you

    in thoughtless stillness
      I see that I already am

...

Withinity Gathering

The Withinity Gathering is a container for community. Along with music and meditation, it invites participants to share and discuss ideas regarding spirituality, from the conventional to the unique. It welcomes all faiths, religions, and open-minded perspectives, honoring each individual as an integral part of the whole.

To become involved, please email

withinitygathering@gmail.com

I look forward to connecting with you...

www.withinity.org

Somatic Forgiveness

Somatic Forgiveness is a process intended to alleviate karma and burden based on limited beliefs formed from negative experiences during childhood and past incarnations. Limitations are surrendered to Source to be composted into wellness and then become integrated through awareness, prayer, meditation, intention, perspective, gratitude and forgiveness for all involved.

This reality is upheld by frequency. "In the beginning was the Word, and the Word was with God, and the Word was God." In the Hindu and Buddhist tradition the Aum or Om is the sustaining sound of all creation.

We all emit a particular frequency and attract the same. If our "notes" are generated from a place of limitation and lack, then we receive that same level in regard to money, success, relationship, health, relationship to God, and peace with ourselves. If we clean our instrument so it can resonate at a higher rate, we will then attract a higher frequency experience.

This process is deeply inspired by the teachings and ideals presented by Christ, Mother Mary (Sophia), Buddha, Lao-tzu, Yogananda, Krishnamurti, and many others.

It is also respectfully based on and developed from the work of John Newton www.healthbeyondbelief.com. From there, modifications incorporating a variety of modalities have been added to create Somatic Forgiveness.

The results I have experienced from this work have been incredibly transformative. Over the years, it has provided an actionable step to deal with any and all negative thought and emotion. It also is a method for shifting meaning put on past experiences, leading to resolution and peace with what was and what is. I can truly say, it's all good now.

Any mention of resolving burden in this text, in my opinion, can be attained through this process. It is fast, easy, and effective. It can be done in person, over the phone, or via video chat. It has shown results for both the individual and the group. I feel inspired to share it, because it has been so liberating for me. And although I make no claim as to its effectiveness for others, I believe in it completely for myself.

"clear your burden so we all can see"

www.somaticforgiveness.com

My Story

I have experienced so many amazing adventures and relationships in my life. I've travelled the world as a professional musician, experienced connection to God and nature in the deepest way, and have had beautiful relationships with many, including my wonderful children. However, the first 46 years of my life were filled with much struggle, depression, and suffering.

On March 1st of 2023, I was experiencing a great loss. In the fire of suffering and out of desperation to care for myself, I had the idea to meld my mind with Source. This visual representation of God in my mind's eye is something I have been acutely aware of since an experience in 2010, and has been a frequent focus in meditation since. I believe that everyone can see the Tao (Spiritual Eye/Face of God/Kingdom/Great Mother) when they close their eyes.

In that moment, when I decided to put my mind with God, I was OK. My body was still experiencing the same burning sensation, but emotionally I was at peace. I was able to observe and feel physical intensity, without assigning any negative meaning to the experience. I was liberated from the suffering of the moment.

From then on, I have been almost completely well. As far as I can tell, I have been freed from all negative thought. Amazingly and logically, an absence of negative thought manifests as a lack of negativity in the human experience. My life has been effortlessly blossoming in regard to work, relationship, expression, and connection to God. I have also settled into an almost completely peaceful, confident and fearless state.

There are many paths to peace, but for me, combining The Somatic Forgiveness process with spiritual study (especially Taoism and the teachings of Christ) has been truly liberating. Because this state of being is so amazing, enjoyable and filled with purpose, my highest desire is to share with all.

Therefore, here I Am.

Thank you...

About The Author

John Whooley works as a musician, teacher, composer, author, creative, healing arts facilitator, and piano tuner. He is first generation Irish, having grown up in San Francisco, CA. From 2010-2023, John made his living exclusively as a professional musician, band leader and musical director. In 2023 he began his healing arts practice (Somatic Forgiveness). In 2024 he wrote his first book (Withinity), along with starting his piano tuning business. He leads The Withinity Gathering (both in person and online), and facilitates workshops combining vocal training and Somatic Forgiveness, entitled Liberating the Voice Within.

He is a dedicated family man living with his wife Andrea, and their 3 children - John, Mary and Adam - in Western Colorado, USA.

www.withinity.org
www.johnwhooley.com
www.somaticforgiveness.com
www.westernslopepianotuning.com

Made in the USA
Coppell, TX
03 November 2024